HIST

The

Historic District

DIANE WRAY

Photography by
FRANK OOMS

Historic Denver, Inc.

Dedicated to Eugene Sternberg, whose friendship has enriched my life.

This project was partially funded by a State Historical Fund grant award from the Colorado Historical Society and with the assistance of Historic Denver, Inc., Jeppesen, Maxine E. Johnson, Eugene Sternberg, and the Scientific & Cultural Facilities District.

Scientific & Cultural
Facilities District

International Standard Book Number: 0-914248-51-0
Text © 2004 Historic Denver, Inc.
Photographs by Frank Ooms except where noted.
Photographs by Frank Ooms and
Diane Wray © 2004 Historic Denver, Inc.

Cover photo: The Gilmore House, 1421 East Cornell Place, photograph copyright © 2004 Historic Denver, Inc.

Arapahoe Acres is listed in the National Register of Historic Places.

Published by Historic Denver, Inc.
1536 Wynkoop Street, Suite 400A
Denver, Colorado 80202-1182

Printed by Mido Printing Company, Inc.

Editor: Marlene Blessing
Design and Composition: Cathy Calder, Blonde Ambition

CONTENTS

A VISITOR'S PROGRAM FROM ARAPAHOE ACRES' "REVERE QUALITY HOUSE
EXHIBITION" ILLUSTRATES THE RICKARD HOUSE (PAGE 20).
ILLUSTRATION: ARAPAHOE ACRES HISTORIC PRESERVATION NETWORK ARCHIVE, DONATED BY RALPH EHRET.

ACKNOWLEDGMENTS

Special thanks are due to Eugene Sternberg, Joseph Dion, and Clyde Mannon, whose interviews and original source materials were invaluable to my research; to my long-time friends and associates in historic preservation advocacy, Michael Paglia and Rodd L. Wheaton; and to the friends and neighbors of Arapahoe Acres, past and present, who assisted my labors, and whose love and dedication promotes the neighborhood's remarkable architectural integrity, including Elizabeth Baylinson, Stan and Holly Bonnes, Phillip and Florine Boxer, Kathleen Brooker, Celia Caso, Carleen Christensen, Kris Christensen, Eric Crotty and Byron Nixon, C. J. Cullinan, Rick Duncan, Ralph Ehret, Rita and Larry Ellermeier, Mickey and Sylvia Freed, Barbara Frison, Ted Frison Jr., Brenda Grall, Charlotte Hawkins, Chuck Henning, Chris Henning, Irene Kohan, Peter Looms, Jane Middlebrook, Gil and Sue Mueller, Gloria Muniz, Bill Nelson, Esther and Don Nesbit, Bill Norlin, Rita Owens, Dorothy Orr, Ron and Suzanne Pollard, Dick and Debby Pool, John and Nancy Ragatz, Don and Gayle Reisch, Nan Rickey, Mark Rodman, Yvonne and Phil Russell, Fred and Lu Schroeder, Gloria Shattuck, Yvonne and Dave Steers, Anne Suro, John Voboril, Fred Welch, Paul and Adair West, and Mark Wolfe. Finally, I would like to acknowledge the future homeowners of the Arapahoe Acres National Register Historic District, and to encourage their preservation efforts in perpetuity.

INTRODUCTION

The History of Arapahoe Acres

Arapahoe Acres is a remarkable community of one hundred twenty-four individually unique modern homes. In them, natural stone, brick, block, wood, and glass join in expressive combinations, unified by an austere palette of earth-toned colors and horizontal forms. Broad curving streets and landscaping provide sweeping, parklike views.

The history of this unique residential development provides a glimpse into one of the most vital periods of the twentieth century—the years immediately following the end of World War II. In a very real way, the war itself brought together the individuals who created Arapahoe Acres, as well as providing the aesthetic, cultural, economic, and technological setting for its realization.

The developer and builder of Arapahoe Acres was Edward B. Hawkins, born in 1902 in Denver, Colorado. The son of a native Coloradan and printer, Hawkins grew up in Denver, graduated from East High School, and studied civil engineering for two years at Colorado State Agricultural College, now Colorado State University in Fort Collins.

In 1924, Hawkins moved to Chicago, where he entered the construction trade. He was hired as a building superintendent by Home Builders of America, a firm involved in the construction of houses in LaGrange, Evanston, Wilmette, Winnetka and Skokie, Illinois. Charlotte, Hawkins' future wife, worked at the same firm as a secretary.

During this period, Hawkins began to undertake small general contracting projects. His increasing interest in residential design led him to study firsthand the Chicago-area work of architect Frank Lloyd Wright. Wright had won international acclaim for his Prairie Style buildings in Oak Park, Illinois, where he lived and worked until 1909.

When the Depression stalled home building, Hawkins joined the Civilian Conservation Corps (CCC), an employment program of President Franklin D. Roosevelt's New Deal. With the CCC, Hawkins built roads, fireplaces, and picnic areas throughout the Chicago region.

In December of 1941, after the Japanese attack on Pearl Harbor, the United States entered World War II. In 1942, now married, Edward and Charlotte returned to Denver. For the duration of the war, Hawkins served in a civilian capacity at the Rocky Mountain Arsenal, a federal chemical weapons manufacturing plant.

Hawkins also began to establish himself as a home designer and builder in Denver. He constructed his first house at 14th and Niagara on a lot next to his family home and continued with homes in the 2500 to 3000 blocks of Race, Albion, Ash, Forest, and Glencoe. Between 1942 and 1949, Hawkins built thirty-five individual modern homes in northeast Denver, ranging in price from $10,000 to $23,000. He designed the houses himself, incorporating ideas about modern architecture and modern living from his work and studies in Chicago.

During this period, Hawkins' firm, Construction Products Company, operated a shop at 14th and Harlan, Lakewood, in an old streetcar barn. Under the supervision of shop foreman Clyde Mannon, houses were prefabricated for on-site assembly. Custom aluminum-frame windows were also manufactured for use in Hawkins' own homes and for sale to local architects and home builders.

In August of 1949, Hawkins conceived of developing an entire subdivision, signing an option to purchase a thirty-acre parcel in Englewood, a growing city in Arapahoe County just south of the Denver city and county line. In November of 1949, he completed the purchase of the property for $5,250. The site was on the frontier between Denver and Englewood, surrounded by open, largely undeveloped land. It encompassed the entire area between Bates to the north, Dartmouth to the south, Franklin to the east, and Marion to the west, excepting a single lot at the corner of Dartmouth and Marion.

Englewood was originally homesteaded in 1864 and incorporated as a city in 1904. In 1949, like the entire nation, Englewood was undergoing a tremendous surge of growth as American GIs flooded home from the war. The population rose from 9,680 in 1940 to 28,000 in 1955, making Englewood the fourth largest city in the state after Denver, Pueblo, and Colorado Springs. Record numbers of new building permits were issued. A massive switching system was under construction to bring dial telephones to the city, a new water purification plant was under discussion, and the municipal tramway system was being converted to bus service.

Throughout the country, the postwar construction industry raced to meet the housing demands of returning GIs. Wartime restrictions on the manufacture of consumer products and new construction were lifted. Raw material consumption and factory production, previously dedicated to the American war effort, now refocused on the domestic consumer market.

It was a period of exciting new advances in residential construction. New and improved light metals and plastics came into common use. Synthetic resins revolutionized plywood building products. Traditional materials like wood, masonry, and concrete, re-engineered for more cost-effective wartime erection, found a new place in home building. Prefabrication and other wartime production efficiencies became integral to peacetime construction.

To promote their products in this booming new market, the Revere Copper and Brass Company joined with the Southwest Research Institute, part of the Housing Research Institute, to create a national program to advance "better architect-builder relations and the general improvement of the quality of speculatively built houses." The program solicited proposals featuring quality modern design, which Revere considered more cost-effective and livable than traditional residential design. Participants juried into the program would build ten or more economical, single-family homes designed by a professional architect. Local and national publicity would promote the homes, architects, home builders, and Revere copper and brass products throughout the country.

In order to participate, Hawkins set aside his own design ambitions and hired board-certified architect Eugene Sternberg, who had been recommended to him by the Revere Quality House Program. Sternberg, a professor at the University of Denver School of Architecture and Planning, agreed to participate because of his interest in the creation of socially conscious housing that combined modern architectural design and economical construction.

Eugene Sternberg was born in 1915 in Bratislava, Czechoslovakia. He earned an architectural engineering degree from the Technion, just outside of Prague. Sternberg was pursuing his graduate degree in architecture at Cambridge University in England when World War II broke out. He remained in London through the war, teaching part-time at Cambridge, then joined the firm of Sir Patrick Abercrombie, where he was involved in the rebuilding of housing destroyed by the German bombing of the city.

In 1945, like many European architects displaced by the war, Sternberg and his British wife, Barbara, emigrated to the United States. He had accepted a teaching invitation at Cornell University in Ithaca, New York, but quickly became dissatisfied with Cornell's restrictions on combining an architectural practice with teaching. At the urging of his friend Lewis Mumford, Sternberg accepted a teaching offer from Carl Feiss, Director of the new School of Architecture and Planning at the University of Denver, becoming the school's first faculty member. The first architectural program in the region, it offered a curriculum based on modern materials, techniques, styles, planning, and social concerns at a time when many architectural schools were still based on the traditional, Old World model of the École des Beaux-Arts, focused on classical and historical models.

Sternberg's site and house plans were readily accepted for participation in the Revere Quality House Program, and a program advisor visited Englewood to lay the groundwork for the construction and display of the initial nine homes. On October 13, 1949, after overcoming the objections of the Englewood fire department to its radical street plan, the subdivision design was approved and filed with Arapahoe County and the Englewood Planning and Zoning Commission.

Hawkins formed the General Investments Company and Hawkins Associates, Inc., to finance and build Arapahoe Acres. Charlotte Hawkins served as vice president and managed the business side of the operation. Clyde Mannon and his wife, Barbara, were both partners, with Clyde serving as corporate secretary and construction foreman. In November of 1949, Hawkins borrowed $85,000 from Central Bank to finance the initial construction phase, mortgaging nine of the lots.

During the initial success of Arapahoe Acres, it became evident that Hawkins did not share Sternberg's interest in low-cost, affordable homes. Much to Sternberg's dismay, Hawkins sold the model home for a higher price than they had originally agreed upon. It created a rift between the two men and, in 1950, Edward Hawkins and Eugene Sternberg ended their collaborative relationship. Approximately twenty homes were built on Sternberg's plans, mostly on the Marion Street frontage.

After the departure of Sternberg, Hawkins was free to fulfill his own ambitions as a designer. His homes were built within the original site plan, but to Hawkins, style took precedence over economy. Altogether,

Hawkins was sole designer of approximately seventy homes in Arapahoe Acres, some ranging up to $40,000 in price.

Hawkins was a charismatic individual who inspired great loyalty. To Hawkins, residents were more than mere home buyers—they were partners in his vision of an all-encompassing community of "contemporary" homes. To quote one original Arapahoe Acres owner, "Ed was a fatherly spirit who taught us a lot about design and sophisticated taste." Hawkins took his responsibilities as an educator seriously and was not shy in correcting the ill-conceived design and color choices of homeowners.

In 1951, young architect Joseph G. Dion was hired by Hawkins to assist him in the evenings and on weekends. Dion was involved in the design of approximately thirty-five homes, including his own (page 36).

The Hawkinses' life revolved around the design and construction of Arapahoe Acres. Their total involvement was reflected in their long-term residency in the neighborhood, as they moved from house to house as construction progressed. In 1957, Edward Hawkins completed his final house in Arapahoe Acres (page 92), and he and Charlotte lived there until their retirement.

On November 3, 1998, Arapahoe Acres became the first, and remains

THE NEIGHBORHOOD NEARING COMPLETION IN 1957, WITH DARTMOUTH AT RIGHT.
PHOTO: COLLECTION OF CLYDE MANNON

today the only, post–World War II residential subdivision listed as a National Register Historic District. The nomination for designation, prepared by Diane Wray, was based on the significance of the neighborhood's social, architectural, planning, landscape, and construction-technology history, as well as on its high level of architectural integrity.

Since its inception, Arapahoe Acres' quality of design has attracted artists, designers, architects, academics, musicians, and professionals. Drawn by common aesthetic and intellectual interests, homeowners share a high level of loyalty to the neighborhood and, over the years, many enduring friendships have been made. Dedicated to maintaining the architectural integrity of their homes and the neighborhood's quality of life, many homeowners have committed themselves to historic preservation. Today, an informal community group, the Arapahoe Acres Historic Preservation Network, promotes preservation, sharing neighborhood history and design, material, and construction resources.

Architectural Style in Arapahoe Acres

The homes of Arapahoe Acres reflect two distinct currents of twentieth-century architecture—the International Style (1920s to present) and the Usonian Style (1930s to present). Historically, both styles are related to the work of Frank Lloyd Wright.

History of the International Style. The influence of Wright's Prairie Style (1900–1920) was a dominant force in the development of nearly all modern architecture after its inclusion in the widely influential Wasmuth Portfolio, published in Germany in 1910. It strongly influenced the International Style, which first appeared in Germany and France in the 1920s and was firmly established throughout Europe and the United States by the 1930s.

When the Nazi government outlawed modern architecture in Germany and closed the Bauhaus, the pioneering school of modern design, many of the key figures instrumental in the development of the International Style emigrated to the United States. The arrival of many of the founders of the International Style movement was integral to the ultimate triumph of the style in the United States during the first decades after World War II.

The International Style is the ultimate expression of two distinct yet interrelated concepts: functionalism and reductionism. Functionalism is the tendency to generate the design of a building as a product of an analysis of functional criteria. Reductionism is the tendency to reduce the elements in a building's design to their most basic expression, resulting in an architecture of stark simplicity.

Sternberg's work is most strongly related to the International Style as seen in the work of Marcel Breuer. Breuer was a first-generation student who later taught at the Bauhaus. He emigrated to the United States in 1937, teaching and practicing architecture with Walter Gropius, the Bauhaus founder who had been appointed Director of the Architecture Department at Harvard.

History of the Usonian Style. His architectural practice diminished by the Great Depression of the 1930s, Frank Lloyd Wright turned to social philosophy and planning. He conceived of decentralizing an increasingly urban America in favor of low-density communities governed by a social, political, and economic system that Wright referred to as "Usonian Democracy." His Usonian Style of architecture reflected his social ideals: the buildings were designed for economical construction and to be energy efficient within their specific climate zone.

The Usonian Style is based on Wright's concept of naturalism. Each architectural project is seen as having a "natural" solution derived from its function and site. Naturalism is, in this sense, closely associated with functionalism. The influence of traditional Japanese architecture is also seen in the Usonian Style. Both styles share open floor plans, flowing interiors with movable screen partitions, an abundance of natural light, overhanging eaves, and shallow-pitch roofs.

Hawkins' and Dion's work in Arapahoe Acres was most heavily influenced by their admiration for Wright's Usonian Style.

Stylistic Characteristics. Both the International Style and the Usonian Style reflect a cubist conception of volume, often displaying multiple blocks of varying form and scale massed within a single building. Axial symmetry is abandoned in favor of asymmetrical composition. Both styles are overwhelmingly horizontally oriented.

In both styles, flat roofs predominate. The International Style also includes butterfly roofs and the Usonian Style, low-pitch gabled roofs. Walls are eaveless or the roofs extend out to form deep eaves that cantilever over the walls beneath. In the International Style, the cantilever dramatizes the horizontality of the building. In the Usonian Style, it also functions to provide shelter and climate control.

In both styles, windows are not simply glass-filled openings in walls. Glass is used as a continuation of walls in other materials, or in some cases, where large expanses of floor-to-ceiling glass or corner windows appear, form the wall itself. Bands of ribbon windows emphasize horizontality. Narrow vertical or small square windows punctuate walls, often serving a decorative function. Window size, scale, and form are often determined in response to the site, the orientation of the building, or on the need for maintaining privacy, views, light, warmth, or protection from heat. Both styles incorporate functional sunscreens and louvers which are also decorative elements. In the Usonian Style, multiple windows are often combined to form simple geometric compositions.

In the International Style, buildings were most often designed in highly finished industrial materials such as concrete, aluminum, and glass and were most often monochromatic, frequently white. Where more natural construction materials were utilized, they were painted, stuccoed, or finished to an industrial appearance. In Arapahoe Acres, however, due to its residential setting, the International Style is softened by the use of natural materials and earth-toned colors more closely associated with the Usonian Style.

In the Usonian Style, natural materials such as wood, stone, and brick predominate. Glass and concrete block also appear, but are detailed and finished to integrate with the natural finishes. Materials are often combined and dramatically juxtaposed. Raked, horizontal masonry joints and the use of horizontal lapboard emphasize the horizontality of the buildings. Usonian Style buildings display a broad palette of earth-toned colors. Brick and natural stone are exposed

PROJECTING ELEMENTS OF THE ROOF STRUCTURE FORM DECORATIVE DETAILS IN THE LANDSCAPE (PAGE 32).
PHOTO: DIANE WRAY

and wood and concrete block are painted in matching or complementary earth tones. In both styles, the same materials used on the building's exterior reappear inside as interior finishes and extend outward, sometimes forming defining elements of the surrounding landscape.

In the International Style, there is no ornament save the joining of materials and forms. In the Usonian Style, materials often formed a key decorative element: Simple, geometric ornament of rectangles, squares, and triangles also appears. In Arapahoe Acres, however, the forms and decoration usually associated with the Usonian Style are often abstracted into a more austere aesthetic more closely associated with the International Style. In both styles, because the ornament is inherent in the materials and the manner in which they are joined, the quality of the design, materials, and craftsmanship is especially important.

The International Style and the Usonian Style share many stylistic features. In Arapahoe Acres, the differences between the International and Usonian Styles become even more indistinct. Each house in Arapahoe Acres can be regarded as a point on a stylistic continuum, with the International Style at one end and the Usonian Style at the other.

The few houses that display direct Japanese influences are anomalies that reflect Hawkins' personal exploration of historic Japanese architectural forms.

THE TOUR

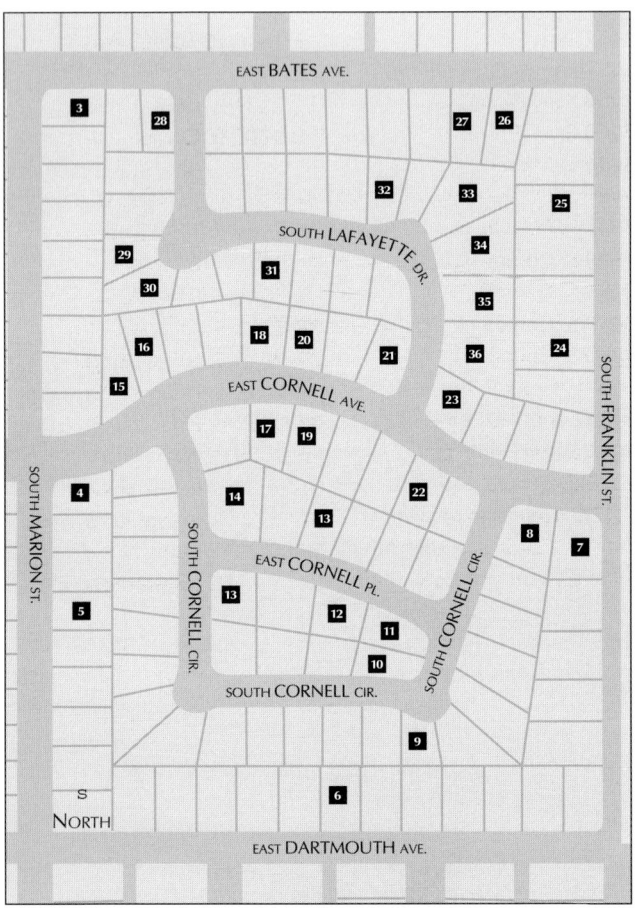

Every single Arapahoe Acres home is different and makes its own unique contribution to the fabric of the neighborhood. The houses on this tour have been chosen as representative examples.

KEY

1   Site Plan
2   Lot Plan
3   2900 S. Marion St.
4   3000 S. Marion St.
5   3030 S. Marion St.
6   1421 E. Dartmouth Ave.
7   3001 S. Franklin St.
8   1520 E. Cornell Ave.
9   3058 S. Cornell Cir.
10 3059 S. Cornell Cir.
11 3069 S. Cornell Cir.
12 1430 E. Cornell Pl.
13 1400 & 1421 E. Cornell Pl.
14 3004 S. Cornell Cir.
15 1313 E. Cornell Ave.
16 1317 E. Cornell Ave.
17 1400 E. Cornell Ave.
18 1401 E. Cornell Ave.

19 1410 E. Cornell Ave.
20 1411 E. Cornell Ave.
21 1431 E. Cornell Ave.
22 1500 E. Cornell Ave.
23 2990 S. Lafayette Dr.
24 2951 S. Franklin St.
25 2921 S. Franklin St.
26 1510 E. Bates Ave.
27 1500 E. Bates Ave.
28 2901 S. Lafayette Dr.
29 2915 S. Lafayette Dr.
30 2919 S. Lafayette Dr.
31 2931 S. Lafayette Dr.
32 2930 S. Lafayette Dr.
33 2950 S. Lafayette Dr.
34 2960 S. Lafayette Dr.
35 2970 S. Lafayette Dr.
36 2980 S. Lafayette Dr.

ARAPAHOE ACRES SITE PLAN
ENGLEWOOD, COLORADO

Designed: 1949
Planner: EUGENE D. STERNBERG

Arapahoe Acres' unique site plan offers pleasant views, privacy, safety, and quiet for residents. Combined with the location of individual houses on their lots, the site plan provides a continuous, unified landscape that showcases the immense variety of the houses.

Sternberg's site plan was founded on his training with the firm of Sir Patrick Abercrombie, a key architect of London's 1944 Green Belt plan. It was unconventional, standing in stark contrast to the surrounding neighborhoods.

Instead of leveling the lots, common practice at the time, the natural grade, which drops forty feet from east to west, was retained. Some houses were sited on flat lots atop high points or low expanses below. Some stepped up or down to the front, rear, or side of their lots.

The neighborhood's rectangular perimeter fit within the adjacent street plan. On the interior, a curvilinear layout violated the surrounding grid, reducing traffic speed and discouraging through traffic. The streets were largely consistent in width, but on Lafayette and South Cornell Circle they widened to form semicircular corners or culs-de-sac. This is most prominent at the west end of Lafayette, where a small landscaped island appears. "Hollywood" sidewalks with integral curbs and gutters create a clean consistent transition between street and drive by eliminating curb cuts.

Unlike adjacent neighborhoods of the period, there are no alleys within Arapahoe Acres. Deliveries and garbage pickup are made on the streets, increasing backyard privacy and security. All garages and carports face the street.

Neighborhood street signs, custom-designed by Hawkins, feature the community's logo. The initial capital letter "A"s are represented by arrowheads, a reference to the Arapaho Indian tribe that once ranged through Englewood.

CUSTOM STREET SIGNS DISTINGUISH
THE NEIGHBORHOOD.
PHOTO: DIANE WRAY

THE PRIVATE PARK IN STERNBERG'S INITIAL
SITE PLAN WAS ELIMINATED BY HAWKINS IN
THE INTERESTS OF PROFITABILITY. INSTEAD,
CORNELL PLACE WAS ADDED AND
CORNELL AVENUE SIMPLIFIED TO A
CONTINUOUS CURVE FROM EAST TO WEST.
ILLUSTRATION: COURTESY OF THE DAILY JOURNAL/
McGRAW-HILL CONSTRUCTION PUBLICATIONS

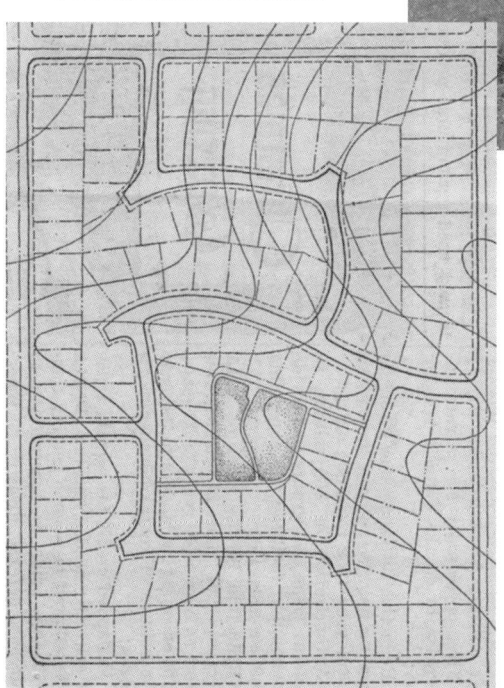

ARAPAHOE ACRES LOT PLAN
ENGLEWOOD, COLORADO

Designed: 1949
Planner: EUGENE D. STERNBERG

   To keep design and construction costs to a minimum, most residential developments of the period had similar lot and house sizes, and limited the number of home plans that were available. As a result, the family size and income levels of home buyers were similar and the neighborhoods represented a very homogenous socioeconomic group. In Arapahoe Acres, a more diverse community of families of varying size and financial resources was envisioned. Lot sizes varied from 66 x 100 feet up to 80 x 150 feet. Homes, ranging in size from 800 to 2,500 square feet, were originally planned to sell from $10,000 to over $20,000.

   Altogether there were 124 lots, 50 on the perimeter and 74 on the interior. The perimeter lots tended to be largely rectangular and consistent in size and shape. Lot shapes on the interior were more varied, including trapezoids and eccentric polygons that responded to the curved, asymmetrical street pattern.

   Homes were set on their lots at twenty-three- to forty-five-degree angles to the street behind a twenty-five-foot building line. They were carefully oriented for privacy and to take the best advantage of southern and western exposures for solar heating and mountain views. Throughout the neighborhood, houses were grouped, designed, and arranged to provide visual continuity, with no individual house dominating its neighbors.

   Paving and house design responded to individual lot size, shape, and grade. Custom-designed fences, gates, walls, and staircases divided the public from the private areas of the lots. Outdoor features were formal when visible from the street and informal in less prominent or private areas of the yard.

   Expansive front lawns featured plantings of deciduous and evergreen shrubs and trees, many dramatically pruned into symmetrical or asymmetrical forms. Specimen rocks and water features also played a key role in the landscape.

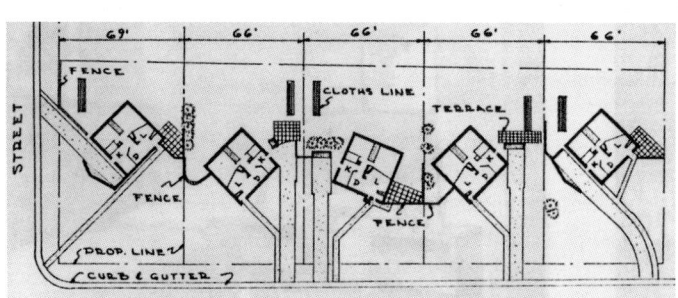

(TOP) CAREFUL POSITIONING OF THE HOUSES IN RELATION TO THE CURVING
STREETS PROVIDES SWEEPING PARKLIKE VIEWS AND THE IMPRESSION OF
A LARGE, PRIVATE ENCLAVE. (BOTTOM) STERNBERG ANGLED AND SET HOUSES
BACK FROM THE STREET TO CREATE ARAPAHOE ACRES' DISTINCTIVE LANDSCAPE.

PHOTO: DIANE WRAY
ILLUSTRATION: ARAPAHOE ACRES HISTORIC PRESERVATION NETWORK ARCHIVE,
DONATED BY EUGENE STERNBERG.

RICKARD HOUSE
2900 SOUTH MARION STREET

Built: 1950
Architect: EUGENE D. STERNBERG

The Rickard House is the original Arapahoe Acres show home, located on the northwest corner of the neighborhood. The grand opening was Sunday, March 12, 1950. Despite an untimely snowstorm, over 4,000 visitors were drawn by headlines that promised comforts normally reserved for more expensive homes.

Visitors were asked to fill out a four-page survey on house design, siting, options, and pricing. One question asked visitors to choose between Cape Cod or Colonial houses and a modern house economically designed for maximum livability and space utilization. Another asked potential home buyers to choose between built-in storage units, stoves, or refrigerators and furniture, or freestanding appliances supplied by the homeowner.

Sternberg selected model home furnishings by Herman Miller, Knoll Associates, and Artek that were lent by Cabaniss, the first store in Denver to sell modern furniture. This included the work of designers Aalto, the Eameses, Nelson, the Knolls, Saarinen, Nakashima, and Le Corbusier. The fireplace, which Sternberg considered essential to comfortable family living, featured a copper finish above.

The kitchen displayed the newest in appliances, including an Amana frost-free freezer-refrigerator and an automatic clothes washer that was concealed by a hinged countertop when not in use. The modular Universal Select-a-Range system allowed homeowners to customize the arrangement of their kitchen stove, oven, and cabinets. In addition to the copper finish on the fireplace hood, other Revere-manufactured products included the pots and pans displayed in the kitchen, copper water pipes, weatherstripping, and window flashing. There were solid brass locksets on the doors and chrome-plated brass fixtures.

The Rickard House is the first of the nine houses completed as part of the Revere Quality House Program. By the time the Denver press announced the neighborhood's grand opening, this first group of

THE RICKARD HOUSE OPENED
FOR PUBLIC INSPECTION ON SUNDAY,
MARCH 12, 1950.

houses had already been sold. Though Sternberg and Hawkins had originally agreed on an $11,500 price tag, the Rickard house sold for $13,500.

The house is located at a forty-five-degree angle to the street on a largely level corner lot. A front-to-back, low-pitch gable roof shelters the simple, one-story form, which includes both living spaces and an open one-car carport. Two angled wall planes create a projecting, prowlike form at the carport, accessible from the east. The formal entrance lies at the end of a walkway that angles across the yard and runs the length of the west elevation.

The house is constructed of red Roman brick masonry, with windows and panels of standard brick rising from the sill line to the roof. Clerestory windows appear beneath the eaves of the carport. A battered Roman brick chimney appears over the roof.

The first owners of the house were Orvis D. Rickard, a salesman for the Rio Grande Company, and his wife, Evelyn, a secretary in the Denver Public Schools.

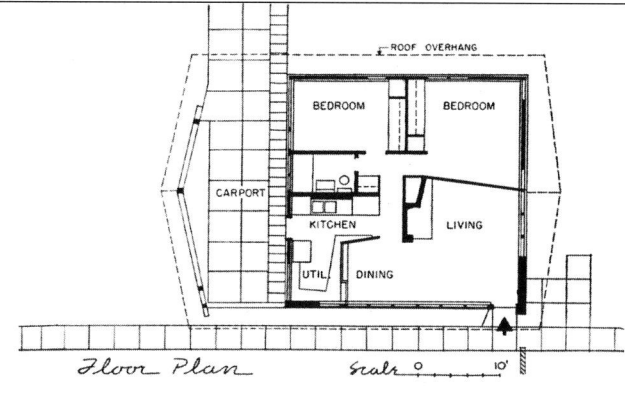

DESIGNED ON A FOUR-FOOT MODULE,
THE FLOWING LIVING AND WORK AREAS WERE SET
APART FROM THE BEDROOMS FOR PRIVACY.
ILLUSTRATION: COURTESY OF *PROGRESSIVE ARCHITECTURE*

THE LIVING ROOM DISPLAYS
MODERN FURNISHINGS AND REVERE
COPPER ON THE FIREPLACE.
PHOTO: GUY BURGESS,
COURTESY OF *PROGRESSIVE ARCHITECTURE*

MASS HOUSE
3000 SOUTH MARION STREET

Built: 1951
Architect: EUGENE D. STERNBERG

The variety of roof forms is a key element in the architectural diversity of Arapahoe Acres. The simplest roofs are a single flat or tilted roof plane, also known as a shed roof. More complex are single roofs formed by two or more angled planes, all low in pitch to maintain the visual horizontality of the neighborhood.

The Mass House features a butterfly roof, so named because it resembles the open wings of a butterfly. It is placed side to side on the body of the house, displaying the form of the roof to Marion Street. It is asymmetrical, the two roof planes joined off-center at their lowest point. According to Sternberg, one intended benefit of the butterfly roof was to capture snow to help insulate against winter heat loss.

The small house is very simple in form, a single rectangular volume that incorporates enclosed living areas and an open carport, sheltering the formal entrance to the house. The primary exterior material is a standard salmon-colored brick.

Facing Marion is a recessed bay of three floor-to-ceiling windows that extend from grade to the sloped eave. The panel next to the center wall of the house is divided horizontally into five panes, of which three are fixed and two are operable. The chimney is flush with the facade, the simple fascia extending across it to emphasize the roofline.

The carport wall steps down, visually connecting the wall to grade. Behind the carport on the north elevation, ribbon windows run beneath the narrow eaves. Simple decorative fences extend from the northeast and southwest corners of the house.

A GRACEFUL SIDE-TO-SIDE BUTTERFLY ROOF IS THE DEFINING
ARCHITECTURAL FEATURE OF THE MASS HOUSE.

THE FRONT-TO-BACK BUTTERFLY ROOF AT THE OWENS HOUSE,
1400 BATES, DISPLAYS ITS FORM ON THE SIDE
OF THE HOUSE, FACING LAFAYETTE.

PHOTO: RON POLLARD

WILSON HOUSE

WILSON HOUSE
3030 SOUTH MARION STREET

Built: 1950
Architect: EUGENE D. STERNBERG

As a result of Revere Copper's publicity campaign, Arapahoe Acres appeared nationally in the architectural and construction press. In 1951, a *Life* magazine article featured the Wilson House in "Modern Living: Best Houses under $15,000."

The basic building block of house design in Arapahoe Acres is a rectangular volume. Its proportions establish the predominant horizontality that is characteristic of the neighborhood.

The Wilson House, like almost 70 percent of the houses in Arapahoe Acres, is one story in height and located on a largely level lot. It is composed of two volumes joined at an angle to create a simple, dynamic composition. The closed volume at left shelters the living areas of the house, a total of 860 square feet. The volume at right is an open carport with built-in storage shed behind.

The fenestration, or window arrangement, forms the house's main decoration. Five large vertical panes with transom windows above align with the main entrance door and transom at left. The northwest side of the house features a ribbon window, a continuous horizontal composition of transparent and blind windows above a high sill line. The design of the windows, in combination with the location of the house on the lot, ensured privacy from the adjacent homes.

The original owners were Dr. W. Errol Wilson, a physician at Colorado General Hospital, and his wife, Eunice.

THE TWO SMALL VOLUMES THAT FORM
THE HOUSE AND CARPORT ARE JOINED
AT AN ACUTE ANGLE.

6

FISH HOUSE
1421 EAST DARTMOUTH AVENUE

Built: 1951
Designer: EDWARD B. HAWKINS

In Arapahoe Acres, the front porches so common to older neighborhoods do not appear, since outdoor entertaining, socializing, and recreation were intended to take place in private backyards. Backyard living was emphasized in a 1955 *Denver Post Empire Magazine* article featuring the Fish House.

The Fish House was designed by Hawkins as one of eight adjacent homes. The group, similar in scale but varied in design, starts at 1321 and extends eastward to 1441 Dartmouth. The houses are linked by concrete block masonry walls that visually unify the homes, emphasize their dominant horizontality, and shelter the backyards from the street. Such masonry walls, wood fences, and gates were important neighborhood features and were often custom-designed for individual houses.

Within backyards, formal patios or terraces for living and entertaining were commonly adjacent to indoor living or dining rooms and kitchens. They were often sheltered by an extension of the house roof or were recessed within the body of the house itself. Patios often included built-in tables and seating and masonry barbecue grilles. Bedroom patios for private relaxing and play areas for children also appeared.

Service areas of the yard were segregated from outdoor living areas. Located in side yards or defined by partition fences or storage sheds, they housed clotheslines, garden tool storage, and garbage cans and incinerators.

The Fish House is the simplest type of house in the neighborhood, a single flat-roof volume incorporating both the living area and garage. The chimney originally featured the neighborhood's only example of weeping mortar, a masonry detail that became more common in subsequent years.

James L. Fish, a distributor for the Clarke Sanding Machine Company, and his wife, Elizabeth, originally owned the house.

Concrete block walls link
the Fish House with its
neighbors to the east and west.

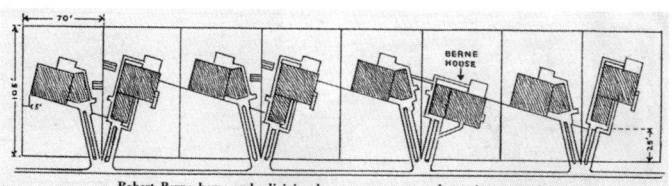

Robert Berne home and adjoining houses are set at angles to improve privacy.

Hawkins designed four pairs of
homes along Dartmouth with
adjoining drives and walkways,
creating broad areas of lawn.
Illustration: Courtesy of the Denver Post

7

BEVILLE HOUSE
3001 SOUTH FRANKLIN STREET

Built: 1955
Designer/Architect: EDWARD B. HAWKINS/JOSEPH G. DION

The Beville House's distinctive stone is pink rhyolite, handpicked by Dion in Castle Rock, Colorado. It features a battered wall, planter box, and canted eaves, all providing a dynamic, decorative contrast to the overwhelming horizontality of the house.

On the facade, unusual decorative wood brackets rest on the masonry wall, appearing to support the deep eaves. The stone wall extends beyond the house to the lot line, forming a garden wall that separates the front and rear yards. The wall is battered, or angled inward as it rises, in opposition to the angled fascia of the roofline. The roof fascia has a smooth surface. The closed soffit is set slightly back and below, creating a distinctive shadow line.

On the northwest corner of the house, stone masonry forms a low battered planter beneath a corner window.

Vertical board-and-batten siding covers the garage wall and flush doors, continuing around to the formal entrance, where the living wing and the garage join. The sidewalk to the front door is sheltered by the cantilevered eave of the garage roof. The entrance, slightly recessed into the body of the house, features a notable custom mail and package delivery box.

On the north elevation, a light screen constructed of wood covers a large window that faces the street.

Driveways in Arapahoe Acres were occasionally stained red like that at the Beville House. All drive and walkway paving was smooth-finish concrete except for decorative exposed-aggregate paving at the two Japanese-styled houses—2980 Lafayette and 3051 Franklin.

This is the second house commissioned by original owners Eugene L. and Koe R. Beville. Their first house appears on page 46.

ANGLED ROOF FASCIA PROVIDE A LIVELY
CONTRAST TO THE HORIZONTALITY
OF THE HOUSE.

THIS SCREEN SHIELDS A LARGE WINDOW
FROM TRAFFIC ON FRANKLIN STREET
AND CORNELL AVENUE.
PHOTO: DIANE WRAY

8

MIDDLEBROOK HOUSE
1520 EAST CORNELL AVENUE

Built: 1954
Designer: EDWARD B. HAWKINS

The multilevel Middlebrook House is distinguished by its complex massing on a sloping corner site. The house presents a largely blind face to Cornell Avenue as it enters the neighborhood from the east. The entrance and the majority of the windows on the house face the interior of Arapahoe Acres to the west and south.

The house is composed of a two-story block and one-story volume that shelter the living areas. Another one-story volume to the south forms the carport, which shelters the main entrance to the house. Multiple flat roofs emphasize the horizontality of the composition.

The two-story section of the house is constructed largely of stack-bond concrete block masonry with flush mortar joints. A prominent lapboard fascia surrounds the roof. Asymmetrical window compositions with spandrel panels of vertical wood siding appear to the south. On the west elevation, a balcony with a canted lapboard fascia appears at a second-story window, terminating at the projecting north wall. Ribbon windows and vertical siding are featured on the north elevation.

The roof fascia narrows on the two one-story wings. Trios of columns support the south wall of the carport, rising from a sandstone planter box. Roof elements extend beyond the body of the house to form decorative garden elements.

A concrete block wall emerges from the center of house, forms the rear wall of the carport, and extends into the landscape to form a retaining wall that divides the front and back yards.

The original owners of the house were Gardner Middlebrook, a medical researcher, and his wife, Jane, who still resides in the house today.

(TOP) LARGE WINDOWS ARE ORIENTED TO FACE THE NEIGHBORHOOD'S INTERIOR.
(BOTTOM) CLERESTORY WINDOWS PROVIDE PRIVACY FROM
CORNELL AVENUE, A THROUGH STREET.
BOTTOM PHOTO: DIANE WRAY

9

COLLINS HOUSE
3058 SOUTH CORNELL CIRCLE

Built: 1953
Designer: EDWARD B. HAWKINS

When roof planes project beyond the walls of the house, they serve a practical as well as aesthetic function. The depth of the eaves, in concert with the size and position of the windows below, control the light and solar heat that reaches the interior. On the Collins House, the depth of the eaves ranges from four inches on the east to almost four feet on the south side of the house. In summer, when the sun is high in the sky, direct sunlight does not reach the interior. In winter, when the sun is low in the southern sky, it floods the house with sunshine and solar heat.

The prominent roof fascia forms an important design detail of the house, emphasizing its horizontality. The underside of the projecting eaves or soffit is closed, finished in plywood panels with a row of circular holes that provide visual interest and serve as ventilation. Many other Arapahoe Acres houses have open soffits that expose the structure of the roof plane. Throughout the neighborhood, both open and closed soffits display an immense variety of detailing, creating a primary decorative element.

Horizontal wood lapboard siding is a primary construction material. It appears as a continuous finish on the roof fascia and on the east wall of the house. The south elevation features vertical panels of horizontal lapboard, aligning with the windows above.

The Collins House is composed of two volumes, one housing the living spaces and the other a one-car garage, set slightly back from the front of the house. It is one of a series of related homes that appear on the south side of South Cornell Circle.

Marvin E. Collins and his wife, Ruth, were the original owners. Collins was the office manager of Toncray Equipment and was an accomplished amateur tennis player.

DEEP EAVES SHELTER A ROW OF WINDOWS WITH VERTICAL PANELS
OF HORIZONTAL LAPBOARD BELOW.

PHOTO: DIANE WRAY

DION HOUSE
3059 SOUTH CORNELL CIRCLE

Built: 1956
Architect: JOSEPH G. DION

In 1951, Edward Hawkins hired young architect Joseph Gerard (Gerry) Dion to assist him in the evenings and on weekends. The two men had been introduced by Eugene Sternberg, with whom Dion had studied architecture at the University of Denver. Though Dion was employed full time at the prestigious Denver architectural firm of Fisher and Fisher, he took the job with Hawkins in order to earn a down payment for his own home in Arapahoe Acres.

Dion, born in 1921 in Lowell, Massachusetts, had become familiar with the Denver area while training with the 87th Mountain Infantry Regiment at Camp Hale, Colorado. After completing World War II service with a combat engineers battalion in the Philippines, he studied under Sternberg and earned his architectural degree at the new University of Denver School of Architecture and Planning.

Dion, like Hawkins, was heavily influenced by Frank Lloyd Wright's work. At the University of Denver, he had helped organize and serve as a student host for Wright's 1948 visit to the school.

Altogether, Dion was involved in the design of approximately thirty-five homes in Arapahoe Acres, including this house, his own residence. The primary materials are stack-bond concrete block and a narrow vertical wood siding. The front entrance is recessed in a shallow, open entrance courtyard. Large angled beams sometimes project beneath the narrow fascia, depending on the orientation of the volumes. A series of narrow vertical windows decorates the facade.

At the time he and his wife, Alba, moved into the neighborhood, Dion was employed at the Denver architectural firm of Stanley E. Moore.

DION (LEFT) AND FELLOW ARCHITECTURE STUDENT MAX SAUL MEET FRANK LLOYD WRIGHT AND HIS WIFE OLGIVANNA AT DENVER'S UNION STATION.
PHOTO: DONALD F. WIEDERSPAN

NARROW VERTICAL WINDOWS PUNCTUATE
THE STACK-BOND CONCRETE BLOCK MASONRY.

THE BOXER HOUSE
3069 SOUTH CORNELL CIRCLE

Built: 1955
Designer/Architect: EDWARD B. HAWKINS/JOSEPH G. DION

The Boxer House was featured in an article in *House + Home* magazine, which revealed the house's floor plan, including an outdoor patio situated between the house and garage. The patio is concealed by a brick wall that makes it indistinguishable from the enclosed spaces of the house. As a result, the house appears even longer and lower than other one-story homes in Arapahoe Acres.

What appear to be three exposed projecting beams are actually decorative extensions of a simple arbor structure that furnishes the concealed outdoor patio to the rear.

The Boxer House is remarkable for the simplicity of its design and its total privacy from the street. Its primary entrance door is flanked by two large floor-to-ceiling panes of patterned glass. Two narrow floor-to-ceiling windows appear at the north and southeast corners of the house. A secondary entrance exits the house at the garage where it steps back from the facade of the house.

The masonry is red Norman brick laid running bond with raked horizontal mortar joints. On the facade, the masonry wall stops below door height. Ribbon windows and plywood panels appear above, beneath deep cantilevered eaves. The closed soffits are finished with board-and-double-batten siding.

To the west, where the flat roof steps down and back to the garage, the fascia narrows. The wall and door of the garage are flush board-and-batten wood siding. The landscape, with sculptured pines, crushed and natural stone, and a red Japanese maple, was the work of Mich Yoshimura, Stanley Yoshimura's son.

Original owners Phillip and Florine Boxer still live in the house. Boxer, Dean of Liberal Arts Emeritus at Metropolitan State College of Denver, was co-owner of Boxer's Steak House at the time the couple moved into the neighborhood.

THE BOXER HOUSE,
A LONG NARROW VOLUME
SET PARALLEL TO
THE STREET, HAS A
NOTABLE MICH
YOSHIMURA LANDSCAPE.

A TRIO OF PROJECTING
BEAMS ENLIVENS THE
SIMPLICITY OF THE HOUSE.

POOL HOUSE
1430 EAST CORNELL PLACE

Built: 1955
Designer/Architect: EDWARD B. HAWKINS/JOSEPH G. DION

The Pool House is a single, long horizontal volume with a side-to-side low-pitch gabled roof and prominent clerestory windows.

Beneath gabled roofs such as this, clerestory windows are angled or raked to follow the pitch of the roof, while the sill remains level. Located above a long wall of Roman brick, these windows provide complete privacy to the living room, while retaining sweeping views of the sky and treetops. Several hopper windows allow ventilation.

The west side of the facade features a window composition of partial height windows, formed by a band of transparent and blind windows set within a wall of vertical siding.

The eaves have open soffits, the exposed beams extending slightly below the line of the fascia. A canopy cantilevers over the main entrance, supported by the front wall and a series of three load-bearing columns. These columns, and a second decorative trio to the east, serve as secondary volumes that add visual interest to the house.

At the far east end of the house, a one-car garage is set behind a perpendicular secondary entrance. The garage wall and door, a single panel that pivots upward, are finished with the same vertical wood siding, creating a visually continuous surface. A simple metal handle rotates to operate the latch mechanism and serve as a handle to lift the door.

Original owners of the house were Dick Pool, employed at the family-owned Spray Coffee and Spice Company in Denver, and wife, Debby, who served with distinction in several educational posts at the local and state level. Debby now resides in another house in Arapahoe Acres.

Three decorative wood columns
adorn the facade, mirroring the
three uprights that carry the
entrance canopy.

A similar detail appears
at the Finch House,
3031 South Franklin, where
the columns mark the recessed
entrance to the house.
Photo: Diane Wray

13

WAGNER AND GILMORE HOUSES
1400 AND 1421 EAST CORNELL PLACE

Built: 1954
Designer: EDWARD B. HAWKINS

The Wagner and Gilmore Houses share similar chimney features that form much of the houses' charm.

Adjacent to the entrance, the east elevation of the one-story Wagner house has a low wall of sandstone with windows above. On the north elevation, the wall increases in height, then angles out from the body of the house to form a triangular firebox, stopping short of the roof. A ribbon window appears above and behind. In front of the windows, a round concrete flue extends from the firebox and penetrates the overhanging eaves. To the west, a contrasting wall of stack-bond concrete block completes the masonry of the facade.

At the Gilmore House, a similar firebox is located at the juncture of the two volumes of the house, but it is rectangular and constructed of red brick. On both houses, the vertical thrust of the chimney is moderated by the overlapping, horizontal roof fascia.

The larger Gilmore house is composed of a two-story block with attached one-story wing, both sheltered by flat roofs. A second major feature of the house is a two-story window composition with an asymmetrical arrangement of a fixed-pane and blind window above a wide louvered spandrel panel and fixed and operable window below.

The original owners of the Gilmore House were Thomas P. Gilmore of the Sheet Metal Union and his wife, Marguerite, a stenographer. The Wagner house was originally owned by Raymond H. Wagner, a salesman, and his wife, Mary, who worked at the Air Force Finance Center.

A TRIANGULAR FIREBOX OF
RED LYONS SANDSTONE
WITH CYLINDRICAL CONCRETE
FLUE APPEARS AT THE
WAGNER HOUSE.

THE CHIMNEY AT THE GILMORE HOUSE
HAS A RECTANGULAR FIREBOX
OF RED BRICK.

IRISH HOUSE
3004 SOUTH CORNELL CIRCLE

Built: 1953
Designer/Architect: EDWARD B. HAWKINS/JOSEPH G. DION

The Irish House is composed of a central two-story section, a one-story wing at the second-story level to the south, and a one-car garage at street grade to the north. Each has a flat roof with a simple, stained wood fascia. The relationship between these roofs and the entrance forms an important detail of the facade.

The fascia of the garage roof extends across the house's facade between the first and second floor windows, ending at the front door, where it shelters the entrance and carries a simple recessed lighting fixture. The roof of the two-story section overhangs the roofs of the wings below. On the ground floor, a wood planter box appears between the windows and louvers, mirroring the line of the roof fascia above and leading the eye to the main entrance.

The main entrance aligns with the end of the second story above. The grid of the screen door frames the twenty-four bull's-eye lights in the door behind. Immediately south of the entrance, a dramatic curved retaining wall emerges from the body of the house.

On the one-story wing at the second-story level, panels of glass, louvers, and plywood alternate above low brick walls. At the southwest corner, the wall extends into the landscape. At the southeast corner the wall projects to form a low garden wall that divides the side from the rear yard. The roof extends beyond the house to shelter the rear patio.

The landscape includes beautiful sculptural pines and a naturalistic waterfall fountain installed by the current owner. Both reflect the tradition of Japanese-style gardens in the Arapahoe Acres neighborhood.

The first owners of the house were Dr. Ernest L. Irish, a dentist, and his wife, Mildred.

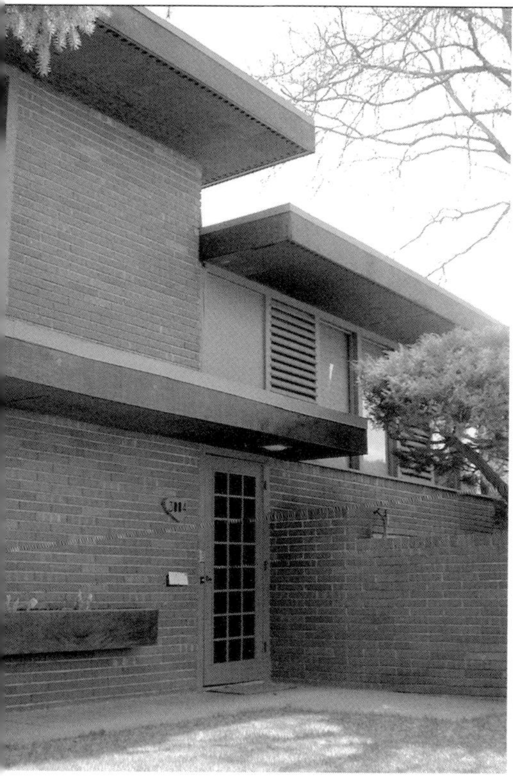

PROJECTING AND EXTENDED ROOFLINES CREATE ARCHITECTURAL INTEREST ON THE FACADE AND DRAW THE EYE TO THE FRONT ENTRANCE.
PHOTO: DIANE WRAY

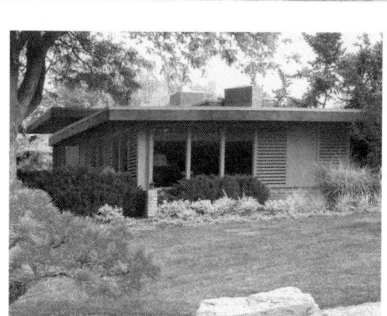

FIXED GLASS WINDOWS, BLIND WINDOWS, AND LOUVERS FORM A WINDOW COMPOSITION ABOVE A LOW MASONRY WALL.

15 BEVILLE HOUSE
1313 EAST CORNELL AVENUE

Built: 1952
Designer: EDWARD B. HAWKINS

Volumes are joined in a variety of ways to create the houses of Arapahoe Acres. The planes that form these volumes provide another level of design diversity.

Wall and roof planes are distinguished by their shape, contour, and dimensions. They are rectangular, trapezoidal, and polygonal, flat and curved, thick and thin, open and closed.

Planes also join and interrelate with each other in different ways. Projecting planes are most common, when wall and roof planes extend beyond the body of the house, softening the distinction between the structure and the landscape.

At the Beville House, one wall projects beyond the body of the garage to form a wing wall. The roof, almost flush with the face of the garage, projects out over the side walls by varying distances. The front of the house extends to form the gracefully curving plane of the garden wall, which separates the front and back yards. On the interior, a curved wall that forms the major decorative feature of the living room mirrors the curving garden wall.

The Beville House is constructed primarily of vertical wood siding and a red Roman brick. This brick, longer and narrower than standard brick, reinforces the horizontality of the house.

On the facade, a ribbon window or narrow horizontal window composition, provides privacy from the street. Behind the garden wall, in the private areas of the lot, floor-to-ceiling windows and glass doors open onto patios from multiple rooms.

Eugene L. and Koe R. Beville commissioned two houses in Arapahoe Acres, the second of which appears on page 30. Eugene was an officer of the U.S. National Bank.

WALLS OF ROMAN BRICK MASONRY
EXTEND BEYOND THE BODY OF THE
HOUSE INTO THE LANDSCAPE.

A DETAIL SHOWS THE PROJECTING
WALL AND ROOF PLANES SO TYPICAL
OF THE NEIGHBORHOOD.
PHOTO: DIANE WRAY

16

SCHWARTZ HOUSE
1317 EAST CORNELL AVENUE

Built: 1952
Designer: EDWARD B. HAWKINS

Window compositions play a major ornamental and functional role in the houses of Arapahoe Acres. They are formed by a variety of transparent and solid components.

The most common of these components is glass secured in a fixed wood frame. Multiple fixed windows are often grouped together, forming geometric compositions that serve as a major decorative element of the homes.

Other transparent windows are operable, consisting of a frame with moveable sash of glass and wood or metal. Operable windows are distinguished by how the sashes function. Casement windows are hinged to the left or right and swing outward, while hopper windows are hinged at the bottom and swing inward.

Less common are awning windows, like those on the Schwartz House, which are hinged at the top and swing outward. A rare example of a fixed metal-frame window also appears on the house, to the left of the entrance.

Fixed and operable glass windows are combined with other elements to form larger window compositions. These include blind windows, or solid panels of wood siding to the left or right of glass windows; spandrel panels or solid panels between vertically stacked glass windows; louvers or panels of fixed, angled horizontal wood slats that allow air circulation in the house without light; and light screens constructed of fixed, angled, vertical slats and installed over a glass window to control light and views. Screens were attached to the inside of operable glass windows, blind windows, and louvers to avoid cluttering the exterior appearance of the house.

Norton N. Schwartz, the owner of Mile High Photography, and his wife, Marian, were the original owners.

ONLY A FEW HOUSES
FEATURE METAL-FRAMED AWNING
WINDOWS LIKE THOSE AT THE
SCHWARTZ HOUSE.
PHOTO: DIANE WRAY

17

GRAY HOUSE
1400 EAST CORNELL AVENUE

Built: 1954
Designer: EDWARD B. HAWKINS

In Arapahoe Acres, the houses are formed by massing large primary volumes. Smaller, secondary volumes enrich and vary their appearance. Some are functional elements, like chimneys or planter boxes. Others are purely decorative. The number of secondary volumes increases in proportion to the size and complexity of the house.

Multiple elements are often combined to create larger and more complex secondary volumes. At the Gray House, a massive slab chimney is anchored by a connecting planter box that projects out onto the lawn. Both are placed perpendicular to the body of the house, emphasizing the location of the formal entrance.

The body of the house, primarily standard red brick, features a variety of ornamental masonry details. The chimney and planter box, laid running bond, appear beside a contrasting stack-bond wall. On the east wall, at the roofline, selected bricks have been omitted from alternating rows to create a pierced geometric pattern on the wall plane. A header course, with the ends of the bricks exposed, appears on the sill of the house's west wing and along the top of the planter box.

Louvers, most often part of larger window compositions, are panels of fixed, angled horizontal wood slats. Some are merely decorative. Others are backed by screens and hinged panels that open to allow air circulation while blocking light and maintaining privacy. On the Gray house, a full-height louver appears as part of a floor-to-ceiling window composition adjacent to the formal entrance to the house. Small louvers flank a pair of windows of the same size at the second story.

Lloyd G. Gray, a self-employed consulting geologist, and his wife, Darlene, were the house's first owners. The Englewood city directory indicates that the Grays rented the house at 1431 Dartmouth while this home was under construction.

Open brickwork forms a decorative feature of the side wall over the garage.
Photo: Diane Wray

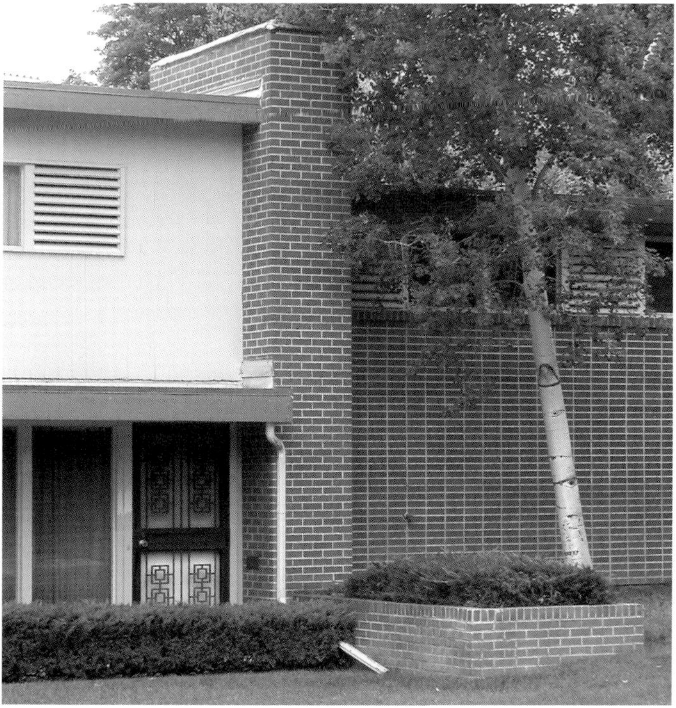

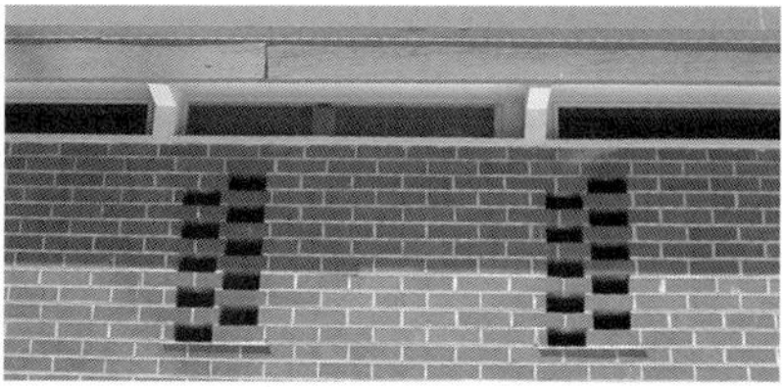

The contrast between running and stack-bond brick masonry creates ornamental interest. Header courses top the planter box and wall.

18

HALPIN HOUSE
1401 EAST CORNELL AVENUE

Built: 1952
Designer: EDWARD B. HAWKINS

Exterior construction materials contribute to the architectural richness of the neighborhood. The most prominent are masonry and wood siding. Some houses have a single type of each; others display multiple varieties in inventive combinations. On many houses, masonry forms the primary material. On others, wood siding plays an equal or dominant role.

In masonry, a wide array of brick, block, and stone in varying colors, textures, and dimensions appears. Variations in bond (the arrangement of the masonry units) and mortar finishes form a primary decorative element of the houses.

A unique masonry combination distinguishes the Halpin House— a narrow brick tile alternates with rows of concrete block to form raised horizontal bands. An accent wall projects perpendicular to the facade at the front door, where the original screen door picks up the horizontal detailing of the masonry.

The one-story Halpin House has a low-pitch side-to-side gable roof. Clerestory windows rise from two sill heights to the roofline. The higher sill height expresses the more private nature of the interior spaces to the east.

The carport is set at an angle to the house, the side and rear wall clad in vertical board-and-batten paneling. Three beams extend from the carport roof to shelter the walk to the entrance and partially enclose a specimen tree.

Original owner Steven Halpin was a well-known drummer who was employed as an occupational counselor with the Denver Public Schools. His wife, Ruie, was an instructor at the John Robert Powers School.

THE SCREEN DOOR MIRRORS THE
HORIZONTAL LINES FORMED BY
ALTERNATING CONCRETE BLOCK
AND BRICK TILE MASONRY.
PHOTO: DIANE WRAY

THE OPEN CARPORT IS ANGLED IN
RELATION TO THE BODY OF THE HOUSE.

19

McCALLIN HOUSE
1410 EAST CORNELL AVENUE

Built: 1954
Designer/Architect: EDWARD B. HAWKINS/JOSEPH G. DION

Planes of contrasting material and varying visual dimensions are often inventively joined to create dynamic wall compositions. The northeast corner of the McCallin House provides a notable example, juxtaposing what appear to be long, slablike walls clad in vertical wood siding with short, narrow walls of brick masonry.

The multilevel house faces north on a sloping lot, with three flat-roof volumes joined in an asymmetrical composition. To the east is the main two-story block. A one-story wing steps up to the south and west, level with the backyard. A two-car garage projects to the north.

The main entrance combines with a floor-to-ceiling window composition at the juncture of the main two-story volume and the garage. It is adjacent to a simple service door that provides access to the back corner of the garage.

Ribbon windows appear beneath deep, cantilevered eaves, providing air circulation and sky views without direct sunlight. The roof fascia is so narrow as to be indistinguishable from the exposed edge of the roof decking. The ends of the projecting beams are cut at an angle and project beneath the fascia, providing a dynamic contrast to the overall horizontality of the house. Clerestory windows appear below the roofline between the projecting beams.

The original owners of the house were Paul F. McCallin, a physician, and his wife, Irene.

A ROOFLINE DETAIL DISPLAYS CLERESTORY WINDOWS
BETWEEN THE BEAMS.
PHOTO: DIANE WRAY

ANGLED BEAMS PROJECT BEYOND THE ROOFLINE TO CREATE
A DYNAMIC DECORATIVE ELEMENT.

20

FREED HOUSE
1411 EAST CORNELL AVENUE

Built: 1952
Designer: EDWARD B. HAWKINS

Michael Freed moved to Colorado when he was appointed director of the Anti-Defamation League in 1950. His wife, Sylvia, was an accomplished violinist who gave classes to private students, including a number of neighborhood children. The Freeds sought out the modern architecture of Arapahoe Acres, first building this home, then purchasing 1414 East Cornell Place.

In the years following World War II, many in the Jewish community embraced modernism, attracted by the ideals that it represented— the promise of the future's triumph over the travails of the past, its emphasis on the guiding principals of democracy, and its basis in and appeal to the rational and intellectual mind.

Arapahoe Acres welcomed Jewish residents at a time when housing segregation was still common and a large part of Freed's work for the League was fighting housing discrimination.

The Freed House consists of a long, single volume that shelters both the living areas and carport. The formal entrance to the house is within the carport. It has an asymmetrical side-to-side gabled roof. Red sandstone planters flank the entrance to the carport. The front wall of the house is a large window composition. At the living room, there are tall windows with a narrow window band below and clerestory windows to the sloping eaves above. To the east, the windows rise over a horizontal band of louvers.

A HISTORIC VIEW OF THE FREED HOUSE SHORTLY AFTER ITS COMPLETION
IN 1952. THE LARGE WINDOW WALL COMBINES FIXED AND
OPERABLE WINDOWS AND LOUVERS.
PHOTO: GUY BURGESS, COURTESY OF THE *NAHB CORRELATOR*
(NATIONAL ASSOCIATION OF HOMEBUILDERS)

21

REED HOUSE
1431 EAST CORNELL AVENUE

Built: 1954
Designer/Architect: EDWARD B. HAWKINS/JOSEPH G. DION

The Reed House features a dramatic formal entrance one and one-half stories in height. It includes a sidelight with decorative colored panels, original house numbers, and a metal mail slot. A large transom window over the door showcases a decorative ceiling fixture that hangs in the entrance hall behind. Though neighborhood paint colors were largely earth tones, the front door is painted coral. Such bright jewel tones were often used to highlight entrances.

Secondary entrances most often appeared on the side or rear elevations of houses, providing formal access to outdoor entertaining and living areas. Even though they are commonly concealed in private areas of the yard, they are also carefully detailed with sidelights, transoms, screen doors and, often adjacent to kitchens, built-in milk boxes. Since the Reed House is located on a large corner site, a secondary entrance is visible on Lafayette. It features a remarkable screen door that reflects the geometric patterning and color panels of the primary entrance.

Immediately adjacent are a pair of garage doors. This is one of only a few houses where the garage entrance does not appear on the facade. The garage wall and doors are made of flush vertical wood siding, resulting in an apparently seamless simplicity integral to the architectural design of many homes.

The Reed House has two perpendicular two-story volumes recessed a half-story below grade, both with low-pitch gabled roofs. A balcony and tall planter box add complexity to the basic volumes of the house.

The house was designed for Homer E. Reed, one of Denver's premier men's clothiers, and his wife, Virginia. The Reeds commissioned Stanley K. Yoshimura to design and execute a spectacular rear garden with waterfall and stream. A small bridge crosses to an open arbor, which is designed to serve as a teahouse.

A SECONDARY ENTRANCE FACING
LAFAYETTE DRIVE FEATURES THIS
SCREEN DOOR.

22

ORR HOUSE
1500 EAST CORNELL AVENUE

Built: 1955
Designer: EDWARD B. HAWKINS

The Orr House is located on a lot that rises to the east and south. At the center is a two-story flat-roof volume that features the neighborhood's only appearance of vertical stack-bond concrete block with raked vertical joints. Two casement windows separated by a plywood spandrel panel form full-height vertical window bays on the north and east elevations. These details provide vertical accents that contrast with the overall horizontal form of the house.

From the driveway to the west, a concrete staircase with Roman brick planter steps up the face of the house. The staircase rises to an entrance landing where the two-story volume joins the one-story wing to the east. The wing's front wall is framed by the projecting roof and side walls. It is faced with vertical board-and-batten siding that is recessed behind an open screen. This screen is one of a handful in Arapahoe Acres. It is a rare example of an ornamental element that does not also serve a functional purpose, designed solely to cast a shifting geometric pattern on the wall behind as the sun moves across the sky.

To the west, the flush vertical siding of the garage wall and door extends beyond the house to the lot line, forming a garden fence.

The Orr House was featured in the *Rocky Mountain News* in 1956 for the way that Hawkins merged the interior of the house with the backyard, using the now-ubiquitous sliding glass door. The version that appeared in Arapahoe Acres had one fixed and one sliding panel with an aluminum and clear plastic door handle. A photo included a rare backyard feature that still survives today—a free-standing shelter for entertaining with a handsome custom wall screen.

Original owners were Warren E. Orr, the directory sales manager for Mountain States Telephone and Telegraph Company, and wife, Dorothy, a nurse.

THE ORR HOUSE DISPLAYS VERTICAL STACK-BOND CONCRETE BLOCK
AND A DECORATIVE WALL SCREEN.

AT THE ROLLER HOUSE, 2901
FRANKLIN, A SIMILAR SCREEN
COMBINES WITH OPEN EAVES.
PHOTO: DIANE WRAY

23

McCOY HOUSE
2990 SOUTH LAFAYETTE DRIVE

Built: 1955
Designer: EDWARD B. HAWKINS

Prominent bandleader Clyde McCoy and his lead singer and wife, Maxine, commissioned this house, the couple's first permanent home after years on the road. It was featured in a *Denver Post Empire Magazine* article in March of 1956, produced by *Post* writer Bettie I. Lopez, an Arapahoe Acres resident who lived with her husband, Louis, at 1341 Dartmouth.

The house was nicknamed the "Sugar Blues" house in reference to Clyde's 1931 hit song by the same name. More famous today is the Clyde McCoy Wah-Wah pedal, an electronic device that mimics a characteristic sound of McCoy's muted trumpet, most famously employed by rock guitarists Jimi Hendrix and Eric Clapton.

The McCoy House is a good example of the larger and more luxurious custom homes that Hawkins began to build in the neighborhood's later years. It was 1,665 square feet, with two bedrooms. Hawkins designed the house, guided by a large book of clippings, pictures, and sketches of homes that the McCoys had admired over the years. Clyde Mannon was credited with the design of the custom built-ins.

The entrance hall featured the dark-stained Philippine mahogany paneling that appeared throughout the main rooms of the house, together with a skylight and built-in planter box.

The predominant color in the living room was "pumpkin," including the upholstery on a twenty-one-foot-long, four-piece sectional sofa. In the dining room, a china closet was concealed in the wall behind a door with a touch-latch. The door itself matched the vertical mahogany paneling, creating the visual impression of a seamless wall.

The "Sugar Blues" den, which featured publicity posters, records, and 125 pounds of scrapbooks full of newspaper clippings documenting the McCoys' career, was a precursor of the media rooms of today. There were black-out drapes, a built-in screen, and an adjoining projection room for storing and playing slides, movies, records, and tapes. The

THE OPEN ROOF PERMITS LIGHT TO REACH THE CLERESTORY WINDOWS
AND PLANTER BOX BELOW.

THIS HISTORIC VIEW SHOWS THE ORIGINAL FLOOR-TO-CEILING
LIVING ROOM WINDOWS.
PHOTO: COURTESY OF THE *DENVER POST*

room's turquoise color scheme appeared on the rug, the Formica top of Clyde's built-in desk, and the cushions on the built-in corner sofas.

The living room and den both featured indirect lighting, with fluorescent fixtures concealed above a wide valance of Philippine mahogany that surrounded the room eighteen inches below the ceiling.

The pumpkin color scheme also appeared in the master bedroom. In the kitchen, pink was used to brighten the mahogany cabinetry. In the bathroom, a custom planter appeared over the vanity and a custom wood trellis held towels.

Sliding glass doors led to the outdoor terrace from the master bedroom, dining room, and hallways outside the den. The house sheltered the terrace on three sides.

In an informal service area of the yard, pets Trumpet, a boxer, and Jet, a dachshund, had their own "contemporary" house with a heating system and picture window.

The house sits on a prominent interior site at the foot of Lafayette. The living areas were to the south, with an integral two-car garage to the north. Beneath the floor-to-ceiling living room windows, the floor slab extended beyond the body of the house to form a design feature on the exterior. A slab chimney extended above the roofline behind the eaves, just in front of the wall plane. Next to the chimney, the roof is opened to allow light to reach a row of ribbon windows and planter box below.

AN *EMPIRE MAGAZINE* ARTICLE (TOP) SHOWS
CLYDE MCCOY WORKING AT HIS DESK WHILE
WIFE MAXINE RELAXED IN THE "SUGAR BLUES
DEN." (BOTTOM) THE LIVING ROOM FEATURED
DISTINCTIVE INDIRECT LIGHTING AND A
FIREPLACE OF STACK-BOND ROMAN BRICK.
PHOTOS: COURTESY OF THE *DENVER POST*

24

BECKER HOUSE
2951 SOUTH FRANKLIN STREET

Built: 1955
Designer: EDWARD B. HAWKINS

A number of houses in Arapahoe Acres are designed to accommodate lots that fall to the rear of the site, but few display this configuration as clearly as the Becker House.

The house is two stories in height, the upper story level with street grade. The driveway drops from the street to the base of the carport, which is level with the lower floor.

A concrete walkway runs from the sidewalk, parallel with the driveway. Flanking the walk are a freestanding brick masonry wall and a low masonry planter box. A short run of concrete stairs descends to the main entrance of the house, sheltered in the carport.

The roof extends from the body of the house over the carport, supported by a series of wood columns to the south and a large enclosed storage unit to the west. The southeast corner of the carport roof is cut back to allow light to reach its interior. Like most carports, the structure of the roof is exposed beneath.

The house has open soffits, the exposed beams tapered to fit behind a narrow fascia. The detailing of exposed beams and rafters in relation to the roof and fascia is an important feature of houses with open soffits. As here, the length of the beams may be tapered or notched. The end of the beams may be fully or partially concealed behind fascia of differing heights. Beams may also extend to partially penetrate fascia, or extend below the fascia. In some cases, a portion of the roof surface may be entirely removed, and the beams or rafters entirely exposed. Finally, the ends of exposed beams may be square, angled or rounded.

The original owners were George W. Becker, a partner in the Denver Ironrite firm, and his wife, Frances Jean.

THE DESIGN AND MASSING OF THE
BECKER HOUSE CLEARLY REFLECT THE
GRADE OF THE LOT, WHICH SLOPES
DOWN FROM EAST TO WEST.
PHOTO: DIANE WRAY

25

HAWKINS/DAVIS HOUSE
2921 SOUTH FRANKLIN STREET

Built: 1955
Architect: HUGH STUBBINS ASSOCIATES

As the neighborhood matured, Hawkins, a consummate promoter, built two *Better Homes and Gardens* display homes in Arapahoe Acres: the 1954 "Home for All America" at 2901 South Franklin Street and the 1955 "Idea Home of the Year" at 2921 South Franklin.

These exhibition homes were related to the original "Revere Quality Houses" in Arapahoe Acres. But instead of soliciting designs, *Better Homes and Gardens* magazine conducted surveys of readers and staff to produce specifications for a trend-setting, cutting-edge house, then commissioned its design. Variations were often created to respond to different geographic conditions. The Hawkins/Davis House was designed by architects Hugh Stubbins Associates of Cambridge, Massachusetts. The "Home for All America," designed by architect Robert Little of Cleveland, was built in over 100 locations in 37 states and Canada.

Like the Revere program, *Better Homes and Gardens* created these homes to promote the magazine, the builders, construction vendors, furnishing suppliers, and other local and national advertisers. Home openings were highly publicized, staged events. In Arapahoe Acres, Lenny Baylinson, Hawkins' friend and organist at Denver's Brown Palace Hotel, offered live music on a Baldwin Organ to model home visitors. The Daniels & Fisher department store provided interior design and furnishings. Almost 3,000 people visited the "Idea Home" on opening day and total attendance was around 17,500.

The house consists of a single large rectangular volume with a low-pitch, side-to-side gable roof. A flat-roof garage wing projects to the north. The house features many of the same details and materials that Hawkins used throughout the neighborhood.

The Hawkinses were the initial residents of this and five other houses in Arapahoe Acres. The first other owners were E. W. Davis, the manager of Denver Beverage, and his wife.

PART OF THE EXTENDED ROOFLINE
SHELTERS THE ENTRANCE; PART IS OPEN
TO LIGHT THE PLANTINGS BENEATH.

AT 2931 FRANKLIN, EXPOSED AND
PROJECTING ROOF DETAILS ARE ROUNDED.
PHOTO: DIANE WRAY

26

MOORE/CHANDLER HOUSE
1510 EAST BATES AVENUE

Built: 1955
Designer: EDWARD B. HAWKINS

Secondary volumes such as masonry planter boxes, chimneys, and accent walls were often constructed of the same materials as adjacent walls. In other cases, contrasting materials were used. The Moore/Chandler House is distinguished by three accent walls of patterned block, adding visual interest to the concrete block and wood siding that form the body of the house.

The largest panel creates a privacy and light screen for the formal entrance, set parallel to the main door. A smaller panel of patterned block is set perpendicular to the street between the two garage doors. The third and smallest panel appears at the far edge of the driveway, parallel to the street. The walls appear to carry the secondary volume of the balcony above.

Other contrasting details include the red sandstone planter box that extends west from the entrance and the prominent balcony, finished in horizontal wood siding.

The Moore/Chandler House is a rectangular two-story volume partially recessed into the hillside behind. The backyard is level with the second story. A naturalistic landscape with informal stone steps leads from the driveway up to the backyard.

The city directory lists multiple original owners for the house: Colorado Supreme Court Chief Justice O. Otto Moore and his wife, Ruth; KLZ radio announcer Warren L. Chandler and his wife, Loahna; and a Rose M. Dye.

PATTERNED BLOCK WALLS, A RED SANDSTONE PLANTER BOX,
AND PROMINENT BALCONY FASCIA SERVE AS DECORATIVE
ELEMENTS OF THE HOUSE.

27

POUND HOUSE
1500 EAST BATES AVENUE

Built: 1955
Designer/Architect: EDWARD B. HAWKINS/JOSEPH G. DION

The Pound House displays a number of window compositions that are characteristic of flat-roofed houses in Arapahoe Acres.

Narrow vertical floor-to-ceiling windows, each composed of two operable casements, appear at the second story, two on the north elevation and one at the north corner of the west elevation. Clerestory windows appear at the roofline, between the exposed beams, cut square and flush just behind the simple, narrow fascia. A ribbon window runs the length of the garage wall just beneath the second story.

The house occupies a sloping lot on the north perimeter of Arapahoe Acres, set at an angle to the street. The second floor of the house, which includes the primary living spaces, projects over the first floor to the west, sheltering the house and garage entrances beneath. The front wall of the first floor steps down to the driveway, forming a base for a single metal column that supports the extended corner of the second story. A broad concrete block chimney rises on the west elevation, the roof extending around it to shelter a patio in the backyard at the second-story level.

The entrance is set in a concrete block wall that emerges from the rear wall of the garage, perpendicular to the garage door. It extends to form a retaining wall for the rear garden, then angles forward and steps down to form a series of planters adjacent to the driveway.

The house is largely constructed of stack-bond concrete block and narrow vertical tongue-and-groove siding. Perry E. Pound, a lease broker with E.N. Murray Company, and his wife, Lola, were the original owners.

(TOP) THE UNIQUE MASSING PLACES THE GARAGE DOOR PERPENDICULAR TO THE STREET. (BOTTOM) CASEMENT WINDOWS ARE HINGED AT THE SIDE AND SWING OUTWARD.

PHOTO: DIANE WRAY

28

CARPENTRY SHOP/BAYLINSON HOUSE
2901 SOUTH LAFAYETTE DRIVE

Built: 1950/1957
Architect/Designer: EUGENE D. STERNBERG/EDWARD B. HAWKINS

Hawkins streamlined and reduced house construction costs by prefabricating custom millwork and cabinetry in the neighborhood's carpentry shop. This included exterior window and door units and built-in interior features such as bedroom chests, headboards, and closet doors; bathroom cabinets, towel racks, and wall display details; built-in desks and bookcases for dens; built-in couches and sideboards for living and dining areas; and cabinets with pass-throughs and breakfast bars for kitchens.

Originally designed by Sternberg, the carpentry shop was converted by Hawkins to a home for friends Lenny and Liz Baylinson after the completion of neighborhood construction. The Baylinsons had purchased an early Hawkins home in north Denver and had become close friends through their shared interest in music. Hawkins was an accomplished musician, playing the bass viol, saxophone, and banjo. Lenny was the organist at Denver's Brown Palace Hotel.

Though not initially designed as a residence, the house shares many features of the neighborhood, including a low-pitch gable roof and long horizontal lines. The exterior details and finishes, added by Hawkins, are similar to those of his other houses. The design and siting of the home's fences and gates are notable. To the south are a formal, painted fence and gate of the same vertical siding as the house. To the north is a more informal, unfinished fence, also elegant in design. Like all Arapahoe Acres fences, they are good-neighbor fences that present a finished appearance on both sides.

The interior is rich in built-in cabinetry and furniture; Liz was delighted by how little furniture she and Lenny needed to acquire when they moved into the house.

Atypically, the house includes a crawl space, reputed to retain quite a bit of sawdust. All the rest of the houses in Arapahoe Acres were constructed on concrete slabs.

THE ARAPAHOE ACRES CARPENTRY SHOP WAS
CONVERTED TO A HOME AT THE COMPLETION OF
SUBDIVISION CONSTRUCTION.

CUSTOM FENCES AND GATES ARE OFTEN
CONSTRUCTED OF THE SAME WOOD SIDING
THAT APPEARS ON THE BODY OF THE HOUSE.
PHOTO: DIANE WRAY

29

FRISON HOUSE
2915 SOUTH LAFAYETTE DRIVE

Built: 1952
Designer: EDWARD B. HAWKINS

When the Frison family moved to Arapahoe Acres, Barbara and Theodore Frison, an attorney for the Forest Oil Company, were just a few of the many young parents raising children in the neighborhood. Their twins Marilyn and Melinda and sons Theodore Jr. and Douglas grew up in a large community of friends. Snapshots from the early years of the neighborhood show families socializing and sharing holiday and seasonal activities, including Easter egg hunts and winter sledding on the hill on Lafayette Drive.

It was not uncommon during those days to find parents raising two children in an 850-square-foot home. Today the same home is considered just large enough for one. As a result, the demographics of the neighborhood have changed and now consist largely of singles and couples. Community events are still common but they are mostly adult affairs, potluck dinners on the crest of Lafayette Hill or evening meetings to socialize and discuss neighborhood maintenance and restoration issues.

Many long-term residents have stayed in touch over the years and, through a neighborhood Web site partially funded by a grant from the Colorado Historical Society, former residents like Ted Frison Jr. are rediscovering their old home and sharing family photographs.

The concrete block Frison House is one and one-half stories in height with a two-story wing and carport that shelters the entrance. All three elements have flat roofs. The main volume is dominated by a large window bay. The upper row of windows aligns with the carport roof and provides a strong horizontal emphasis to the house. A concrete block wall supports the carport roof to the north, with a row of ribbon windows at the roofline.

A FULL-HEIGHT WINDOW BAY
DOMINATES THE FACADE OF THE HOUSE.

THE HOMES ON LAFAYETTE DRIVE FORM A BACKDROP FOR
TED FRISON JR. AND FRIENDS CA. 1954.
PHOTO: BARBARA FRISON

30

CHRISTENSEN HOUSE
2919 SOUTH LAFAYETTE DRIVE

Built: 1951
Designer: EDWARD B. HAWKINS

During the postwar years, carports and garages became integral to house design, reflecting the growing importance of the automobile in the life of the American family. No longer parked on the street or housed in small, separate garages on alleys, cars now merited their own special accommodations.

In Arapahoe Acres, carports and garages were key elements in house design, often recessed within the body of the house itself. In others they formed separate volumes of the house, sometimes dominating the overall architectural composition.

The Christensen House is composed of a single, one-story volume with a flat roof, sharing a masonry wall with the house to the east. A remarkable two-bay carport, partly original, partly a sensitive addition, extends to the north, facing east.

The roof of the south bay extends from the body of the house and shelters the front entrance, notable for its original custom door, screen door, sidelight, and overhead lighting fixture, all unified by horizontal crosspieces.

The north bay steps out to the east. A column and masonry walls support the prominent roof beams that extend beyond the roof fascia. Ribbon windows bring light into the interior. Custom gates, one in a grid pattern, provide access between the carport bays and the backyard to the west.

The masonry wall of the carport's rear elevation extends into the landscape to form a shared garden wall with the Frison House to the north (page 76).

Norman W. Christensen, a salesman for the Mountain States Telephone and Telegraph Company, and his wife, Carleen, were the first owners of the house.

THE CHRISTENSEN HOUSE SHARES A CURVED MASONRY WALL WITH ITS NEIGHBOR.
BETWEEN THEM, IT BECOMES A GARDEN WALL DIVIDING THE FRONT AND BACK YARDS.

THE CARPORT IS FORMED BY AN ABSTRACT COMPOSITION
OF INTERLOCKING AND OVERLAPPING PLANES.
PHOTO: DIANE WRAY

31

LAZIER HOUSE
2931 SOUTH LAFAYETTE STREET

Built: 1950
Designer: EDWARD B. HAWKINS

"Prefer one story? Two? Undecided? Then try a split-level house!" urged a *Household* magazine article of March 1953 featuring Arapahoe Acres. The article goes on to enthuse about "the many features that made living in a split-level house easier, better, happier" including "the long, low, pleasant lines that we associate with good one-story houses," the quiet and privacy provided by the vertical separation of living and sleeping areas, and the shorter, safer runs of stairs.

To minimize the bulk of larger houses and maintain the overall horizontality of the neighborhood, Hawkins partially recessed two-story sections below grade and joined them with one-story wings, resulting in a number of "split level" homes. This configuration also easily accommodated the change of grade on sloping lots. The Lazier House is an excellent example of this type, which came into common currency in the postwar years.

On the Lazier House, the two stacked volumes to the east are partially recessed below grade and attached to a one-story wing to the west. On the interior, half-flights of stairs move upstairs to bed and bathrooms and downstairs to dens and recreation rooms. Living rooms, dining rooms, and kitchens were commonly located on the main floor.

The original owners of the home were Harry A. Lazier and his wife, Elaine. In 1951, the *Denver Post* and the Denver Association of Home Builders sponsored a "My Favorite Home" contest. Lazier, account executive with the Arthur G. Rippey advertising agency, won top prize for a photograph of this residence.

SPLIT-LEVEL HOUSES EASILY NEGOTIATE CHANGES IN LOT GRADE.

A SIDE WALL FEATURES BOARD-AND-BATTEN SIDING WITH A DECORATIVE ARRANGEMENT OF SMALL PUNCHED WINDOWS.
PHOTO: DIANE WRAY

32

HAGERTY HOUSE
2930 SOUTH LAFAYETTE DRIVE

Built: 1953
Designer: EDWARD B. HAWKINS

After the war, returning veterans were eligible for home loans guaranteed by the Federal Housing Administration (FHA). Under the plan, a veteran could borrow the full cost of a house with no down payment, only a charge to cover fees and loan costs. However, the program also included strict FHA housing design guidelines, which shunned modern homes with flat roofs and plain, asymmetrical facades as a fad, refusing to consider them sound, long-term investments.

Though early homes in Arapahoe Acres had been successfully financed by FHA/GI loans, the FHA balked as Hawkins began to build more extreme modern designs. After much discussion, FHA financing on the Hagerty House was approved, but the valuation was low—only $12,800 on a house with a sales price of $21,000. By 1954, however, conventional private mortgages had become the norm and with the success of the subdivision, Hawkins himself began to provide financing.

The Hagerty House was radical in design, even for Arapahoe Acres. Located on a site that slopes to the west, it has a shed roof that joins two angled side walls of differing heights with projecting triangular dormers. A combined entrance and window composition with red sandstone planter boxes appears near the center of the house. Bands of ribbon windows are also featured. The primary exterior finish is wood siding. A one-car garage is recessed into the body of the house. As might be expected, the interiors of the multilevel house are remarkable, including a large living room, one and one-half stories in height, with an angled ceiling.

The initial owners were Raymond O. Hagerty, an attorney for the Title Guaranty Company, and his wife, Adele.

A HISTORIC PHOTO SHOWS THE HAGERTY HOUSE SHORTLY AFTER COMPLETION.
AN ASYMMETRICAL COMPOSITION OF SHED ROOF AND ANGLED SIDE WALLS
FRAME THE FACADE.

PHOTO: GUY BURGESS, COURTESY OF THE *NAHB CORRELATOR*
(NATIONAL ASSOCIATION OF HOMEBUILDERS)

33

KAEMPFER HOUSE
2950 SOUTH LAFAYETTE DRIVE

Built: 1952
Designer: EDWARD B. HAWKINS

Located near the highest point of the Arapahoe Acres interior, the design of the Kaempfer House reflects the location, elevation, grade, dimensions, and shape of the lot.

The house faces southwest, a two-story volume with a low-pitch, side-to-side gable roof. A two-car garage is recessed within the body of the house at the first floor. On the second story, a wall of windows rises to the roofline above a band of louvered panels, taking advantage of sweeping mountain views.

The side wall, in contrast, is intended to provide privacy for the neighboring houses to the west. The front portion of the wall is solid brick masonry, broken only by an asymmetrical composition that forms an important decorative element of the house.

To the east, the upper story of the house rests on a curving retaining wall of Lyons sandstone. Behind, a staircase rises to the backyard, where a small one-story wing with gable roof projects perpendicular to the second story of the house. The lot's rear boundary is much wider than the street frontage, creating a remarkably large garden to the rear. The masonry is Norman brick, laid running bond, with the vertical joints of one row centered on the bricks above and below. In contrast, the perpendicular accent wall that marks the formal entrance on the side of the house is laid stack bond, with the vertical joints aligned. The contrast between running and stack bond is commonly used as a decorative detail in the neighborhood. Raked horizontal mortar joints complete the masonry details.

Myron A. Kaempfer, a public accountant with his family firm of Kaempfer and Kaempfer, and his wife, Lola, were the house's original owners.

A WALKWAY RUNS PARALLEL TO THE SIDE WALL OF THE HOUSE, TERMINATING AT A PROJECTING ONE-STORY WALL THAT MARKS THE FRONT ENTRANCE.

A NARROW FULL-HEIGHT WINDOW AT THE SECOND STORY FORMS AN ASYMMETRICAL COMPOSITION WITH THE FIVE INDIVIDUAL GLASS BLOCKS BELOW.
PHOTO: DIANE WRAY

34

HAWKINS/PRILLER HOUSE
2960 SOUTH LAFAYETTE DRIVE

Built: 1952
Designer: EDWARD B. HAWKINS

Edward and Charlotte Hawkins lived in this house during the height of construction in Arapahoe Acres. During that period, it also served as the neighborhood's design and sales office. Hugo L. Priller and his wife, Lois, owners of Priller's Dress Shop in Cherry Creek, were the house's first other owners, and members of the family still reside here today.

Priller commissioned the remarkable landscape with waterfall fountain from Stanley K. Yoshimura. An article entitled "Japanese Gardens Come to Denver," in a 1961 issue of the Denver Post Empire Magazine, related: "Yoshimura was in the middle of a commission to landscape a 26-acre California estate when World War II ended the project. He and his family were sent off to a war relocation camp in Arizona, then moved to Denver where he opened a restaurant. A year ago last spring, he felt the time was ripe for his kind of gardens in the Denver area."

The house is two stories with a flat roof. It is partially recessed into the hillside, the backyard level with the primary living spaces of the second story. A window wall on the upper level features mountain views. Below, a two-car garage is recessed within the body of the house.

Secondary volumes add relief and visual interest. Most prominent are the roof and balcony fasciae of horizontal lapboard. The roof fascia wraps around the sandstone chimney. The balcony partially overlaps this chimney to the south and terminates at the projecting side wall to the north. A triangular bay window appears on the south elevation.

The wall planes are sheltered behind the secondary volumes. The north section of the lower wall is concrete block masonry with a band of windows above. Set behind, to the south, is a wall with two flush garage doors, all finished as a continuous surface of vertical tongue-and-groove wood siding. The formal entrance is at the juncture of these two wall sections. The front door, perpendicular to a floor-to-ceiling sidelight of vertical corrugated glass, is pierced by a grid of twenty-four bull's-eye glass lights. Original custom street numbers are intact.

PROMINENT ROOF FASCIA, BALCONY FASCIA, AND A MASSIVE SANDSTONE
CHIMNEY ORNAMENT THE TWO STACKED VOLUMES THAT FORM
THE BODY OF THE HOUSE.

STANLEY K. YOSHIMURA AT
HIS DRAFTING TABLE.
PRILLER HONORED HIM WITH
A SIMPLE BRONZE PLAQUE
IN THE BACKYARD.
PHOTO: COLLECTION OF YO YAMASAKI

35

SITTERMAN HOUSE
2970 SOUTH LAFAYETTE DRIVE

Built: 1955
Designer: EDWARD B. HAWKINS

Many houses in Arapahoe Acres have roof and wall planes that extend beyond the body of the house, blurring the boundaries between the building and the surrounding landscape.

In contrast, the Sitterman House has a framed wall plane, which creates a strong sense of shelter. Evenly projecting side wall, roof, and floor planes are finished to form a continuous frame around the composition of glass and blind windows at the second-story level. A side view reveals the distance that the planes project beyond the body of the house.

The Sitterman House faces west just below the highest point of Lafayette. The house is a single two-story, flat-roofed block recessed into the hillside behind. Though the front wall of the second floor is largely transparent to allow homeowners to enjoy mountain views to the west, the fenestration of the side walls is designed to create privacy for and from neighbors. The handsome board-and-batten siding is punctuated by full-height vertical windows to the north. To the south, a remarkable grouping of square windows lights the kitchen to the rear.

The front entrance is marked by a feature wall of red sandstone, a broad sidelight, and a custom screen door with a strong horizontal emphasis, reflecting the overall composition of the house. A sandstone planter to the right of the door extends to form a retaining wall for the south side yard. At the driveway, a curved staircase of red sandstone rises to the side yard to the north. The garage wall and doors are finished in a continuous surface of narrow vertical siding.

The original owners were Fred W. Sitterman, owner of Fred W. Standard Finance Company and Sitterman Real Estate, and his wife, Dorothy.

THE FRAMED SECOND STORY CANTILEVERS OVER
THE GROUND FLOOR, ITS WINDOWS RECESSED
BACK TO THE MAIN WALL.

A RED SANDSTONE STAIRCASE BETWEEN THE
DRIVEWAY AND SIDE YARD FORMS A
CHARMING GARDEN FEATURE.
PHOTOS: DIANE WRAY

36

HAWKINS HOUSE
2980 SOUTH LAFAYETTE DRIVE

Built: 1957
Designer: EDWARD B. HAWKINS

As the subdivision neared completion, Hawkins decided to locate a neighborhood park and playground on this lot, an idea that Sternberg had originally proposed for another location (see page 17). Neighboring homeowners objected, and in 1955 Hawkins began construction of a home on the lot.

That same year Hawkins, undoubtedly inspired by his studies of the Japanese influence on Wright's work, traveled with Charlotte to Japan. Upon his return, he demolished the partially completed house on South Lafayette and began again. The final version, unabashedly Japanese in style, has many design, material, and landscape features unique to the neighborhood.

These include the traditional Japanese Irimoya roof, basically a hipped roof, sloped on all four sides, with a gabled roof above. The balcony rail is based on a traditional design and the windows at the rear of the balcony have electrically operated shojis. The wood siding on the ground floor is modeled on a traditional Japanese fence form. The front door is modeled on a shoji. An unpeeled birch trunk with applied original street numbers serves as a column to support the corner of the balcony that cantilevers over the formal walkway to the house. The ground floor is dominated by rubble stone masonry.

Numerous Japanese-style landscape and paving features appear throughout the grounds, accompanied by a remarkable collection of specimen trees and formal, meticulously pruned shrubs.

The house was the Hawkinses' residence for ten years prior to retirement and their final home in Arapahoe Acres. In exchange for the loss of the playground, the Hawkinses opened their swimming pool and adjoining pool house to neighborhood families on Saturday mornings during the summer months.

THE HOUSE AND YARD ARE
RICH IN DETAILS REFLECTING
THE INFLUENCE OF TRADITIONAL
JAPANESE ARCHITECTURE AND
LANDSCAPE DESIGN.
PHOTO: DIANE WRAY

CHARLOTTE AND EDWARD HAWKINS
BOARD THE AIRCRAFT FOR THEIR FLIGHT
TO JAPAN CA. 1956.
PHOTO: LENNY BAYLINSON, COURTESY OF
ARAPAHOE ACRES HISTORIC PRESERVATION NETWORK
ARCHIVE. DONATED BY LIZ BAYLINSON.

POSTSCRIPT

As Arapahoe Acres was nearing completion, Edward Hawkins purchased land near Bowles and Belleview for the development of a new project, Arapaho Hills. Before ground was broken, Hawkins withdrew from the project to devote more time to his personal life. Longtime business partner and contractor Clyde Mannon, now working under the name Mannon Associates, assumed the project, with Bruce Sutherland as architect.

In 1967, Edward and Charlotte Hawkins retired to Vista, California, where Hawkins designed and built his final home in a Japanese style on the San Luis Rey golf course. For eight years, the two traveled around the world on tramp steamers. Edward B. Hawkins died in 1991 at the age of eighty-nine. Charlotte died in 1995.

Concurrent with the development of Arapahoe Acres, Eugene Sternberg began "Mile High Cooperative" off Dahlia, just south of Iliff. This was one of the first projects to take advantage of a new federal postwar housing program to provide low-cost loans for cooperative single-family housing. Sternberg designed and supervised the construction of all the homes in Mile High. Its residents, including the

3005 CORNELL CIRCLE
PHOTO: DIANE WRAY

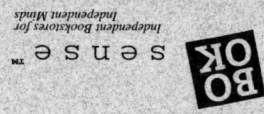

Sternbergs, were largely University of Denver professors, whose modest salaries restricted their access to quality housing. "Mile High" features a central neighborhood park like the one Sternberg originally envisioned for Arapahoe Acres.

After the closure of the University of Denver School of Architecture and Planning in 1952, only six years after its inception, Sternberg was free to devote himself entirely to his architectural practice. With a focus on socially involved projects, including schools, hospitals, medical facilities, and elderly and low-income housing, Sternberg's practice thrived. He designed over four hundred buildings in Colorado, Nebraska, Wyoming, Pennsylvania, Rhode Island, British Columbia, and the United Kingdom. He also continued to design individual homes and plan residential communities. One of these was Orchard Hills in Arapahoe County south of Belleview between South Yosemite and South Dayton Streets. For the one hundred fifty–acre site, Sternberg designed a broad greenbelt, walking paths that adjoin each lot and a neighboring lake, and seven of the original homes. Now retired, Eugene and Barbara Sternberg reside in Evergreen, Colorado.

Gerry Dion continued to work with Hawkins and Clyde Mannon, doing site planning for the Arapaho Hills subdivision. In addition to working for Fisher and Fisher and Stanley E. Moore, Dion worked with the architectural firm of G. Meredith Musick, where he participated in the design of the Denver City and County Jail. He then joined the planning firm of Harmon, O'Donnell and Henninger. After becoming a registered architect in 1960, Dion formed the partnership of Morse, Dion and Champion, which designed the Houston Fine Arts Center, now the home of the Denver School of the Arts, and the Chapel at Colorado Women's College, now part of Johnson & Wales University.

After Morse's death in 1968, Dion returned to Massachusetts, where he worked as an architect and municipal maintenance director. He and his wife, Sally, currently reside in New Hampshire.

Clyde and Barbara Mannon live in retirement in Golden, Colorado, and Hawaii.

SOURCES

BOOKS

Albrecht, Donald, ed. *World War II and the American Dream*. Washington, D.C.: National Building Museum/MIT Press, 1995.

Sergeant, John. *Frank Lloyd Wright's Usonian Houses; Designs for Moderate Cost One-Family Homes*. New York: Whitney Library of Design/Watson-Guptill Publications, 1984.

Wright, Gwendolyn. *Building the Dream; A Social History of Housing in America*. Cambridge, MA: MIT Press, 1983

NEWSPAPERS AND PERIODICALS IN CHRONOLOGICAL ORDER:

The Denver Post
    "Home Builder Honored," circa 1949.
    "'Different' Home Plan to be Shown in Denver," September 27, 1949.
    "Article Lauds Denver Home Builder's Skill," October 30, 1949.
    "Subdivision's First Home Open Sunday," March 9, 1950.
    "Arapahoe Acres Home Project Wins Citation," February 25, 1951.
    "Glass, Stone Featured in Contemporary Home," April 18, 1953.
    "Simplicity of Design Attracts Interest," June 6, 1953.
    "Modern Homes Seen Gaining Popularity," circa 1954.
    "3,000 Persons Visit Model Home Featuring Contemporary Styling," circa August 29, 1954.

Rocky Mountain News
    "New Flat-Type House is Gaining Favor Here," February 7, 1950.

The Daily Journal
    "Arapahoe Acres, New Subdivision, to Be Constructed in Englewood," August 30, 1949.
    "Hawkins' Arapahoe Acres Features Split-Level Contemporary House," February 8, 1952.

Progressive Architecture
    "The Speculative House; Arapahoe Acres: Denver, Colorado," July 1950:78.
    "P/A Case Study; Architecture in Denver, Colorado, 1950–1951," March 1951: 71.

Practical Builder
    "A Sell-Out in Contemporary Architecture," July 1951: 28.

Biographical Index

2950 SOUTH LAFAYETTE
PHOTO: DIANE WRAY